NEW POEMS BOOK TWO

Charles Bukowski

Edited by John Martin

These poems are part of an archive of unpublished work that
Charles Bukowski left to be published after his death.

Grateful acknowledgement is made to John Martin, who edited
these poems.

This edition first published in 2003 by
Virgin Books Ltd
Thames Wharf Studios
Rainville Road
London
W6 9HA

First published in the United States of America in 2003 by Ecco
as *sifting through the madness for the Word, the line, the way*

Published by arrangement with Ecco, an imprint of
HarperCollins Publishers, Inc., New York, New York USA

A catalogue record for this book is available from the British
Library.

ISBN 0 7535 0799 4

Typeset by Phoenix Photosetting, Chatham, Kent

The Random House Group Limited supports The Forest Stewardship
Council (FSC®), the leading international forest certification organisation.
Our books carrying the FSC label are printed on FSC® certified paper.
FSC is the only forest certification scheme endorsed by the leading
environmental organisations, including Greenpeace. Our
paper procurement policy can be found at
www.randomhouse.co.uk/environment

MIX
Paper | Supporting
responsible forestry
FSC
www.fsc.org
FSC® C018179

Printed and bound in Great Britain by Clays Ltd, St Ives PLC

CONTENTS

the way to create art is to burn and destroy
ordinary concepts and to substitute them
with new truths that run down from the top of the head
and out from the heart.

PART 1

the problem with

c
o
n
c
r
e
t

poetry

i

s

the

s

a

m

as the

problem with

c
o
n
c
r
e
t

people

A WISE ASS

that's what I was on campus, some of the professors,
    I'm sure,
feared me or at least preferred that I not be in their
class.
I had a scarred and lean countenance and I slouched
in my seat
hungover and dangerous.
I refused to buy the assigned books or study.
I was insolent, cool and crazy and I drank and fought
    every night.
my parents supported me out of fear.
I was the meanest 18-year-old son of a bitch in the
world.
I would leap up in class and make incoherent
speeches challenging whatever the professor had just
said.
I was a pain in the ass and I thought I was tough but I
    was afraid to
go out for the football team or ask a girl for a
date.
I guess I was crazy.
all I read was Nietzsche and Schopenhauer.
I was taking journalism and art classes and
when they asked us for one writing assignment a
week, I wrote seven.
some said I was a genius.
I felt like a genius or I felt like I thought a genius

should feel.

one day I got in a fight after art class with the
200-pound fullback of the football team.
we fought for 30 minutes on the campus
lawn.
unfortunately nobody stopped us.
I finally won although I never expected to.
I kept waiting to lose and it didn't happen.
then I began to get popular and I couldn't take that so
I pretended to be a born-again Nazi.
then I got a lot of freaky guys full of hate trailing
after me so
I told them to fuck off and I became the school
recluse.
I don't know, after two years on campus I didn't
want it anymore so
I quit and got a job in the railroad yards as a
laborer.
I rented a small room downtown and roamed the
streets at night.
some genius I was, some god-damned
genius!
I made several trips to the *Herald-Examiner* and the
L.A. Times and told them I wanted to become a
reporter.
I never made it past the receptionist's desk.
"fill out these forms," they said.
I shoved them back.
they didn't know I was a genius.

one night in a bar I got in a fight with a little
guy, he must have weighed only 130 pounds.
he whipped my ass.
the next night I tested him once more.
he whipped my ass all over again.

a week later I took a bus to New Orleans.
somewhere along the way I bought a book by
a famous guy called
Hemingway.
I couldn't read it.
the fucking guy couldn't write!
I tossed the book out the window.
a girl on the bus kept staring at me.
she turned in her seat and made a
sketch of my face.
she wrote her address on
the back of the sketch and
got off at Fort Worth.
I went on to Dallas, got off, caught a shave,
showered at the "Y,"
took a bus back to Fort Worth and found her.
I sat in the front room with her while her mother
sat in the bedroom.
we talked a long time, it was great, she was beautiful.
then she held my hand and
started talking about God and I got the
fuck out of there.

I took another bus to New Orleans.

I had a portable typewriter with me.
that's all that I needed
to prove I was a genius.
that, and another 35
years.

THE DRESSMAKER

my first wife made her own dresses
which I thought was nice.
I'd often see her bent over her
sewing machine
putting together a new dress.
we were both working and I thought
it was great that she found the time
to create her own
wardrobe.

then one evening I came home and
she was crying.
she told me that some guy at work
had told her that she had bad
taste in her wearing
apparel.
he had said she looked
"tacky."

"do you think I dress tacky?"
she asked.
"of course not.
who is this guy?
I'll beat hell out of him!"

"you can't, he's my boss."

she cried some more that
evening.
I tried to reassure her and she
finally stopped.

but after that, she purchased
all her dresses.
I thought that
they didn't look nearly as good on her
but she told me that the fellow at work
had praised her new
clothes.

well, as long as she stopped
crying
I was satisfied.

then one day she asked me, "which do
you like best, my old dresses or
the new ones?"

"you look good either way," I
answered.

"yes, but which do you *prefer*?
the old dresses or the new ones?"

"the old ones," I told her.

then she began crying again
and wouldn't stop.

there were similar problems with other
aspects of our
marriage.

when she divorced me she was still
wearing only the store-bought
dresses

but she took the sewing machine
with her
and a suitcase filled with dresses
of the old
kind.

LUNCH IN BEVERLY HILLS

it's a shame, it's a damned shame,
sitting here at this table
spread with a clean white tablecloth,
on a veranda overlooking Beverly Blvd.
a light lunch, you might even say a
business lunch, your lawyer has
collected some money due you from
a movie producer.
your bright energetic lady
lawyer, her assistant and my wife,
we eat and drink wine, and then order coffee and talk
mostly about the impending war
as at all the tables around us
there is more talk about the im-
pending war (although at the table just
behind us some men laugh loudly
so they must be talking about
something else).

I feel very strange, very odd
that we are sitting at this table
spread with an immaculate white
tablecloth with all the successful
people sitting here with us
with the war about to start
tomorrow
or next week
as we sit over wine and coffee

on a beautiful, clear day in
Beverly Hills.

and although I am guilty of nothing,
I feel guilty nonetheless.
I think that I would feel better about every
thing if I was sitting instead in a cheap room
with flies crawling my wine
cup.
not pleasant, of course, but at least it's war of
another kind.

but I am in Beverly Hills and that is
all that there is to
it.

I reach for my gold card as I
twist in my chair and
ask the waiter for the
bill.

SHE WAS REALLY MAD

I love you, she said,
and spit in a bowl of
jello
put it in the
refrigerator
and said,
you can eat that later
for dinner!

then she was gone
like a whirlwind
out the door
in a rush of angry
skirt.

A TREE, A ROAD, A TOAD

a table of 7, all
laughing loudly, again and again,
almost deafening,
but there is no joy in their
laughter, it seems machine
made.
the pretense and falsity
poison the air.
the other diners seem not to
notice.
I am asphyxiated by the laughter,
my gut, my mind, my very meaning
gag on it.
I dream of taking a gun, of
walking over to the table
and blowing their heads off,
one by one.
of course, this would make me
far more guilty than they
are.
still, I have the thought and
then I realize that I expect too
much.
I should have long ago
realized that this is the way
it is:
that everywhere there are tables of 2,
3, 7, 10 or more

where people
laugh meaninglessly and
without joy,
laugh inanely without
real feeling,
and that this is an inevitable part
of all that,
like a tree, a road, a toad.

I order another drink and
decide not to kill them, even
in my imagination.

I decide, instead, that I am a
very lucky man:
the table is twenty feet away.
I could be *at* that table, sitting there
with them,
close to their mouths,
close to their eyes and their ears
and their hands,
actually *listening* to the conversation
which is causing their joyless
laughter.
I have been in many such situations before
and it has been one bloody cross,
indeed.

so, I settle for my good fortune
but can't help but wonder
if there is any place left in the world
with a table of 7 where

there are genuine feelings,
where there is
great and real laughter.
I hope so.
I have to hope so.

IN ONE EAR AND OUT THE OTHER

my father had memorized many sayings that he liked
to
repeat over and over:
"if you can't succeed, suck eggs!"
"my country, right or wrong!"
"early to bed and early to rise makes a man healthy,
wealthy and wise!"

my mother just smiled as he mouthed these
pearls of wisdom.
me?
I thought, this man is a fool.

"any man who wants a job can get one!" was one
of his favorites during the Depression years.

almost everything he said was stupid.
he called my mother "mama."
"mama, we gotta move out of this neighborhood!"
"why, daddy?"
"because I saw one, mama!"
"one what, daddy?"
"a nigger . . ."

another one of his favorites was:
"eenie, meanie, miney, mo, catch a nigger by the
toe, if he hollers make him pay, 50 dollars every
day!"

he never voiced these aphorisms while sitting down
but always while marching smartly about the
house.
"God helps those who help themselves!"
"you listen to your father, Henry," my mother would
tell me.
that poor woman, she meant it.

"don't do as I do," he'd shout, "but do as I
say!"
I ended up doing neither.

and the day I looked down at him in his
coffin
I almost expected him to say something
but he didn't so I spoke up for
him:
"dead men tell no more tales."

thank Christ, I had heard enough.

then
they closed the lid and my uncle Jack and
I went out for hamburgers and fries.

we sat there with the food in front of us.

"your father was a good man," uncle Jack
said.

"Jack," I replied, "good for what?"

EXCUSES

once again
I hear of somebody who is going to
settle down and
do their work,
painting or writing or whatever,
as soon as they get a better light
installed,
or as soon as they move to a new
city,
or as soon as they come back from the trip they
have been planning,
or as soon as . . .

it's simple: they just don't want
to do it,
or they can't do it,
otherwise they'd feel a burning
itch from hell
they could not ignore
and "soon"
would turn quickly into
"now."

BYGONE DAYS

once upon a time men used to wait in
the front room, smoking cigars, drinking brandy
and discussing the important things, the manly
things, as the ladies worked in the kitchen
preparing dinner while we enjoyed the
aroma of spices, the smell of
cooking meat and our conversation.

always, there was plenty of brandy and more serious
    talk.

we had come through some very difficult times
the wars and what-not and
now we were in charge, invincible and very male: our
expectations, our dress, our manner,
we were as lions resting comfortably
in our homes as the feast was
prepared.

it was our just due. no questions asked.

at mealtime we would fill ourselves,
offering up appreciative grunts,
nodding affirmatives to our ladies; we were well fed
    and
well pleased.

then followed the removal of the main course and on
    to the
dessert and the coffee.

that done, the ladies would remove the empty

plates and we would relax awhile over our coffee
as the ladies began washing the dishes in the
kitchen.
"let's go back to the front room," the host would
    finally
say.

there we would switch from brandy to whiskey or
    scotch.
sobered by the meal we lighted fine Cuban
cigars as the sound of running water and the clanking
    of
plates emanated from the kitchen.

yes, the world was exactly as we wanted it to be

until female liberation began and now we are often
found in the kitchen, washing the dishes, and
    sometimes we even have to
cook the meal, too.
the ladies now go cocktailing around 2:30 p.m.,
chatting, gossiping, they get giddy, giggle, and often
are intoxicated. Sometimes they get into tearful
arguments.

the kitchen is forgotten; the ladies are
liberated; they chain-smoke and wear pantsuits instead
    of
dresses; they curse simply as a matter of course;
they toss around words like "fuck" and "shit" and
they are particularly fond of shouting "piss off!"
they spill drinks on themselves, laugh hysterically.

the men are uncomfortable and exchange little side
glances; they say nothing, just as the women used to
do.

the men have given up smoking, and drink sparingly:
they are now the "designated drivers."
the ladies discuss everything: politics, world
affairs, philosophy, art and sundry other matters.

once in a while one of the men will speak out. it will
usually be something about sports, like, "I think the
    Yankees need
a new center fielder."

"what?" one of the other men will say. "I didn't hear
    you."

the ladies are laughing, talking loudly, cursing,
    smoking,
pouring fresh drinks . . .

"what?"

"I said, 'I think the Yankees need a new center
    fielder.' "

"oh yes, I think you're right."

then the men will fall back into a profound silence.

they are waiting for night to fall.

IN A LADY'S BEDROOM

trying to write a poem
in a lady's bedroom
(onions on my breath)
while she cuts a dress
out of freshly bought
material.

I suppose, as material,
I'm not so fresh,
especially with onions
on my breath.

well, let's see—
there's a lady in Echo Park,
one in Pasadena, one
in Sacramento, one on
Harvard Ave.
perhaps one of them would be more interested
in me
than in a dress (for a while,
anyhow).

meanwhile I sit in this
lady's bedroom
by a hot window
while she sits at her
sewing machine.

here, she said, here's a
paper and pen,
write something.

all right, I'll be kind:
some ladies fuck like mink
and dance like nymphs
and some create
nice dresses and lonely poets
on hot July
afternoons.

MODEL FRIEND

Wentworth worked as a model.
he even got paid for it and he didn't
look any different from
the rest of us.

"put on your cap for Hank. show
him how you posed as a sea
captain," said Clara.

Clara was his woman.
I was with Jane.

we were drinking in their apartment,
a very nice place.
we lived in a tiny room
just a few blocks away and were far
behind in the rent.

we had brought along our own wine
and they were drinking it.
I was 40 pounds underweight
barely alive and
going crazy.

Wentworth got his cap and
put it on.
it was blue and flopped just
right.
he stood in front of a
full-
length mirror and smiled.

I was being sued in the aftermath
of a driving accident
had ulcers
and every time I drank whiskey I
spit up blood.

"Wentworth," I told him, "you look
dashing."

why don't they give us something to
eat? I thought. can't they see that
we're starving?

Wentworth turned from the mirror
and looked at me. "modeling is a
good show. what do you do?"

"Hank's a writer," Jane said.

Jane was a good girl: she answered all the
questions for me.

"oh," said Clara, "how fascinating!
how's it going?"

"things are a little slow," I
said.

Wentworth sat down and poured himself
another drink.

"wanna arm wrestle?" he asked me.

"o.k.," I said, "I'll try you."

we bellied up to the table, came to
grips, nodded, and he slammed my arm

on the table
like a marsh reed.

"well," I said, "you were best that
time."

"wanna try another?"

"not right away."

"maybe I can get you into
modeling?"

"what as?"

"or into a secretarial position.
how many words can you type a minute?"

"I'm into longhand right now."

"what do you write about?"

"death."

"death? nobody wants to read about
that."

"I think you're right."

the girls were talking to each other.
then Clara got up and went to the
bedroom.
she was there awhile.
then she came out with a new hat
on.
she stood,
smiling.

"oh, Clara," said Jane, "it's
lovely!"

"women don't wear hats anymore," said
Clara, "but I just *love* hats!"

"you *should*, you look so *dear*!"

so there was Wentworth in his blue sea
captain's cap and there was Clara in her new
purple foxglove.

"wanna try another arm wrestle?" asked
Wentworth. "the best two out of
three?"

"just pour me a drink."

"oh, sorry . . ."

the evening continued and we got to be good
friends, I suppose.
we sang some songs, sea songs among them,
and Wentworth gave me a cigar.
I was proud of Jane.
she had a great little figure, just
right.
even when we didn't eat for days I was
the only one who lost weight
which sometimes gave me the idea that
she might be eating someplace else while I
practiced my new longhand prose style.
but it didn't matter: she deserved the
food.

meanwhile
I begged off the arm wrestling and we
kept drinking my wine.
when it was gone
the evening was over.

I remember standing in their doorway
hugging him and her
saying
goodbye, yes, yes, it was a great
evening.

and then the door closed and
there was the empty street.
as we walked back to our
room Jane said, "look at that
moon! isn't that moon
wonderful?"
I couldn't say it was so I
didn't answer.

then we were standing in the hall of our
roominghouse.
I took out the key
and stuck it in the door and it snapped in
half and the door wouldn't open and the key
wouldn't come back out so I gave the door what
shoulder I had and it split open and
as it did some guy down the hall hollered,
"HEY, YOU GOD-DAMNED DRUNKS, I GOT A
GOOD MIND TO SEND YOU DOWN THE
   RIVER IN A SACK OF SHIT!"

it sounded like mr. big mouth lived in
room 8.

I walked down to room 8 and
knocked. "come on out," I said. "I've got
something for you."

there wasn't any answer.

Jane was at my side. "you've got the
wrong door."

"I've got the right door," I told her.
I BANGED on the son of a bitch.

"COME ON OUT, FUCKER! I'LL KILL YOU!"

"it was room 9," said Jane.
"you got the wrong door."

I walked down to 9 and BANGED again. "COME ON
OUT, FUCKER, AND I'LL KILL YOU!"

"if you don't go away," I heard a voice say
from behind the door, "I'm going to call the
police!"

"you chickenshit scum," I said.

I walked back to our room and Jane
followed me.
she closed the door and I sat down
on the edge of the bed and pulled off
my shoes and stockings.

"your buddy in the sailor cap," I
told her, "he gets on my
nerves."

THE INVITATION

listen, Chinaski, we've always LOVED your work,
we've got all your books, especially the dirty ones, you
just really get the word down and we love you, I love
you, and I just busted up with my old man, he liked
your stuff too, he was the one who introduced me to
your shit and now I'm living with a guy in his pick-
up truck who makes his living at swap meets, he hates
your writing but I hated it too when I first read it,
anyhow the rest of us (and we're some GANG) we've
got this idea, we're kind of Funk City, you know, and
we thought we'd throw a party in CELEBRATION
OF YOU, we don't bow down to too many pricks but
your stuff just tears us up, SO—we got together and
scrounged up a few chips (that's MONEY, HONEY)
and we'll meet you at the airport, we got this great
orange VW for one and then there's Ricky's pick-up,
so there's TRANSPORTATION, and there's a *good*
gang here, plenty of beer and you see we want to
CELEBRATE YOU in the way you deserve and even
tho you're an ugly fuck we can probably (?) line you
up with something young and tender. maybe we can
also fix you up a reading at the local bar, plenty of
cowboys and x-cons who understand where you're
coming from, you gotta be the greatest writer since
Kerouac and so here it is—our invitation—in honor of
ya, come on up and if nobody will lay you my pussy
ain't too dry, ain't too bad, I'm 22 and last month I
went to the Naropa Institute over in Colorado, to

their last fucking function, and I asked, "WHERE'S CHINASKI?" and they acted like they never heard the name, that bunch could make the Sphinx puke, really, so listen, let us know soon!!!!

    love,

        MOONCHILD

PS:

832–4170 (I use the phone at the pharmacy, ask for Larry and tell him ya got a message for the KEEPER OF THE STARS AND BARS, he'll know who you mean!)

HOLLYWOOD HUSTLE

the first one came up to me while I was
eating in the Italian cafe
and he said,
"pardon me, sir, may I read the Home Section
of your newspaper?"
"no," I said, "you may not."

I finished eating and went outside and
another guy stopped me at the corner:
"hey, Jack, can you use a
watch?"
he opened his hand and in his
palm was a
wristwatch. "can't use it,"
I said.

I walked across the street and down a
block and another guy stopped
me. he was carrying 2
pool sticks.
"listen," he said, "I need 50 cents more
to get a meal. and by the way, can I
sell you a pool stick?"

I shook my head,
gave him a quarter and walked
on.

a man shouldn't say "no" all night
long and I just can't shoot a
decent game of
pool.

BUDDHA CHINASKI SAYS

sometimes
you have to take
a step or
two
back,
re–
treat

take
a month
off

don't
do anything
don't
want to
do anything

peace is
paramount
pace is
paramount

whatever
you want
you aren't going to
get
it by
trying too
hard.

take
ten years
off

you'll
be
stronger

take
twenty years
off

you'll
be much
stronger.

there's nothing to
win
anyhow

and
remember
the second best thing in
the world
is
a good night's
sleep

and
the best:
a gentle
death.

meanwhile

pay your gas
bill
if you can
and
stay out of
arguments with the
wife.

LIKE LAZARUS

the unknown time and place of
your death is a
mystery, isn't it?
also the manner of your
death?
you can go while tying a
shoelace
or you can go with a knife
in your belly.

you can go in fear,
you can go in peace,
you can go without being aware
of either.

in L.A. County General Hospital
my ward was next to the
operating room.
I was a poor sleeper
and I was often awake
between 3 and 6 a.m.
and that was when they
wheeled the bodies
out,
bodies covered
with a sheet,
and the doors would swing open
and the heads would
come out first,

then the remainder of
the body
followed,
rolled along by the
white-clad
orderly.

I always counted the
bodies.
one, two, three,
four every blessed
night.

no need for me to
count sheep,
I had something better.

one night they broke
the record (at least
during my sojourn),
they got up to
8.

I waited and waited
for #9
but he/she never
came.

the sun finally came up
however
and the bedpans
were rattled
and the nurses

made grim jokes
and complained of their
domestic
problems.

our ward was a
special ward
where they put the
desperate cases,
we were all
teetering on the
edge
and some of us
finally
went
over,
but the goings
(at least during my
sojourn)
weren't bloody,
ugly or even
dramatic.
there was even
a tinge of boredom
about it
all.

"Mr. Williams, Mr. Williams . . .
here's your breakfast!
Mr. Williams?
Mr. Williams?

Oh, he's
gone . . ."

there was never an
empty bed
for long.
they changed the
sheets and Williams was
replaced by Miss Jones and when
Jones went she was
replaced by
Mr. Wong.

and the sun came
up blazing
in the mornings
just to taunt us
and there was much
time to waste.
we were too far gone to speak
to one another and
the only sounds were
wheezing and
occasional bits of
coughing or
groaning
and every now and then
a weak and pitiable voice
mewing
"nurse . . . nurse . . ."

I left that place, that palace

of death, without looking
back.
I went down the aisle
between the beds
and
then down many
steps
(I didn't count
them)
and out the front
entrance into the
street.

I phoned the cab
from a nearby
bar.
the cab took me over
the bridge,
over the invisible
L.A. River
and we went back
to my part of
town.
It was a crazy feeling
finally
being
out.

I paid the cabby and
went up the
walk.

I still had my key,
I put it in the front door
and opened
it.
the room was on the
second floor,
up a steep
stairway.

the dog met me halfway
up.
he was a big one,
he leaped at me
joyously,
his tail whipping like a
snake on
fire.
I was still weak and
he almost pushed me
over.

I walked on up the
stairway and down the long hall
and into the small
room.

she was sitting on the
couch, smoking a
cigarette and
reading a
magazine.

startled,

she looked
up.

"Jesus, why didn't you
tell me?"
she asked.

"what's there to
tell?
is there any
beer?"

she got up, walked quickly
into the kitchen
with an uneasy smile,
looking back at me
over her
shoulder.

SOFT AND FAT LIKE SUMMER ROSES

Rex was a two-fisted man
who drank like a fish
and looked like a purple anemone.
he married three others
before he found the right one.
they fought over cheap gin
were friendless
and satisfied
and frightened the landlord.
then she began to holler plenty
and he would listen dully,
then leap up red with choice words
until she began again.
it was a good life,
soft and fat like summer roses.

good bedmates
they were
until he got hurt at work, near
fatally, it seemed,
and he stayed in bed then
smiling it off
while she got a job as a waitress
in a cheap café
where the lads were rather rough,
sometimes drunk, slapping her rear while
Rex drank gin in bed while
she walked about, saying nothing,

thinking about a Greek who came in
   mornings,
touched her hand, quietly said "eggs,
eggs again."

Rex continued to drink gin in bed
and one night she didn't come back.
nor the next. nor the next.
and with a lurch, he got out of bed
and walked holding to walls
around and around and around
and fell, clutching the carpet,
saying, "o, Christ! o, Christ!"

the Greek was very different,
he didn't drink at all and
said he believed in God,
he loved diffidently, like a butterfly,
and he had a new refrigerator.

Rex was sitting in bed with the gin
one dark night
when she returned, saying nothing.

"bitch! cheap bitch!" he said as
she sat down on the bed, fully dressed,
and looked pleased to see him.
later he stood upright on the floor,
   smiling and himself again, and
said, "I'm going back to work tomorrow
   morning.
and you, you stay out of that goddamn café!"

IN TRANSIT

the French border guard had a black waxed
mustache and an ivory face with pimples
for eyes.
he stank of perfume and his uniform
was wrinkled but his boots were
new and shiny: the overhead
lights reflected in them and made
me dizzy.
he was frosty, he was filled with a
strange cold rage.

it was only 15 degrees outside
but in that building
with too much heating and all the hot
lights
it must have been
110.

the heat
only maddened the
guard.
little drops of sweat ran down his nose
and dripped off.
he looked dangerous.

"PASSPORT!" he screamed.

I handed it over, smiling blandly at him.

he poked at the photo.

"IS THIS YOU?"

"yes, sir."

"YOU LOOK YOUNGER THAN THIS
PHOTOGRAPH!"

"I was ill when the photo was
taken . . ."

"ILL? WHAT WAS IT?"

"the flu . . ."

"THE FLU?"

I didn't reply.

he opened my suitcase and
began to take the contents
out.
he flung them all about, then
stopped.

"WHAT ARE THESE
PAPERS?"

"paintings . . ."

"WHOSE?"

"I painted them."

he glared at me, his wax mustache
quivering.
then,

"ALL RIGHT. YOU CAN GO
THROUGH!"

I went to work gathering up my
things.

next in line was a voluptuous
young lady.
the guard snatched her
passport, looked at it, then smiled
at her.

I had my suitcase put together
and was leaving
when I heard him:

"*he said he was a painter!*"

then I was out of there and soon
I was out of the building
and into the 15
degrees
and it was so fine and lovely
out there, truly
refreshing.

"DEAR MR. CHINASKI"

I have tried your publisher with my
work.
they didn't understand my poems
and they say their schedule is
filled for now,
so I thought maybe you should read
my manuscript
and then talk to them.
I've also enclosed an envelope for your
response.
I've long been an admirer of your
work,
and I don't want to kiss your ass,
but I consider you one of our
greatest living writers,
so if you would just look over the poems
enclosed, I'll be forever in
your debt.

one of the greatest living writers
read them,
trashed them, including the stamped
and addressed
return envelope.

what a helpless soft son of a bitch!

the way he wrote he
was.

SILVERFISH

"SILVERFISH!" my father would
holler and my mother would come
running with the special can
of spray.

my father was always finding
silverfish.
it seemed to go on for days
and years on
end:
"SILVERFISH!"

I saw a silverfish
now and then
but I never said
anything.

mostly they liked to hang
around the bathtub
or in dark wet
places.

they hardly seemed a
threat
to me.

but my father's hysterical excitement
upon finding a
silverfish
never
abated.

well, it did after my
mother's death
because my father had nobody
to holler at.

then my father died
and in his casket he looked
just like—
you know—
a big one.

but I didn't holler
anything.

THE POPULARITY KID

they are good fellows all, in one way or another,
but they all seem to find you on the same day at
the racetrack, especially when your mood isn't one of
the best.
the first one, you don't remember his name,
he pushes his face real close
and starts talking fast and loud but the meaning
of what he says passes right over your head.
after a bit you
break away from him somehow and maybe there's 15
minutes' peace, then a mutuel clerk catches your
eye, waves you over, he's one big smile, grabs
your hand and pumps it, he's asking about some-
body you both know but it's really about nothing
at all. "have you seen Mike
lately?"
"no, I haven't."
luckily, somebody behind me wants to buy a
ticket and I quickly move away.

a race passes and I am walking along when another
poor soul jumps me, he's all smiles too and he pumps
my hand but doesn't say anything, he just stares,
smiling, smiling.
he's in the horse business and I ask him something
about his horses and when I get the answer
I say, "great!" then spin on my heel and move
off.

just before the last race I am approached by two
complete strangers.
now, I am going to have to say something ugly.
I have absolutely no interest in any of these people
and never would approach them myself.
why do they feel a need for me?
is it cordiality? fear? respect? boredom?

and it's not only the racetrack, it's wherever I
go.
say, in my supermarket, the manager will rush toward
me, his arms widespread.
there is this sushi place, when I enter, the owner will
greet me and bow low.
he does not do this for his other customers.
at a Mexican restaurant I frequent, the owner
always rushes over, slides into my booth, puts an arm
about me and says, "it's good to see you!"
at this Chinese place, the waitresses gather around
my table, chatter, make jokes and expound
little Oriental philosophies.
it also happens to me in gas stations, etc.
I never make the first overture, I always try to keep a
    low
profile but it doesn't seem to help.

what is it?
I don't find myself interesting.
it must be pity, I must look woeful,
at death's door.
but then, thinking back, all this began when I was

about 16 years old, people began trailing me, wanting
to be friends, attaching themselves to me.
granted, many of them were mentally defective,
    but not
all of them.
it was back then when I first began evading
people, hiding from them, finding excuses to
discard them as friends, and it has gone on ever since.

I'm a god-damned magnet to the human herd
and I don't like it and I don't want it and it won't
stop.
I'm just going to have to die to get away and even that
might not work:
the ghouls will come running toward me, arms
    outstretched,
saying, "hey, Chinaski, we've been waiting for you!
we wanna drink beer with you and talk!
just talk and drink beer!
now we can hang out with you
forever, baby, FOREVER!"

DEATH AND WHITE GLUE

the tiny summer creatures are flying
all around here now and
I have nothing to
smoke.

now
all around here
tiny summer creatures fly.
I usually blow smoke at them
and at the lamp bulb
and watch the smoke curl in the air
and sometimes think of things
like
death and white glue.
the summer creatures bite at night
when I am asleep
and in the morning I have bumps on my
body
which are delightful to
scratch.

my love is upstairs watching a comedy on
tv.
down here I am drinking wine
Liebfraumilch
and my love considers this a
betrayal of our love, but
you and I know what a betrayal of love really
is.

meanwhile
I crush some of the tiny summer creatures
some find the white glue
but I leave a few of them
so that I am able to scratch myself in the
morning.

the summer creatures are so strange
I feel that they know me—
one falls into my glass of
Liebfraumilch
I watch him flick and kick about
and then I
drink him down.

I hope that comedy is good
upstairs. I have my own show going on down
here.

FUN TIMES: 1930

Harold was always scared.
he was easy.
we had a good time with
Harold.

we'd pretend to hang him 2 or 3 times
a week.

we had a rope and we'd
corner him on the back porch
of Mrs. Keller's place.
there was a heavy
rafter.
we'd put the rope around
his neck.

"this time we're gonna do
it, Harold, we're tired of
fucking around.
this time we're *really* going
to hang you!"

"oh, no! *please!*"

he would cry silently, the
tears rolling down his stupid
freckled face.

"stop your damned blubbering!
now, if you don't want to die either you
got to drink piss or eat shit!
which do you want?"

Harold would just keep crying.

"which do you want? answer or
we'll hang you now!"

"piss," he would always say.

then we'd piss on him, all over
his shoes and his pants, while
laughing.

then
when his family finally moved out of
the neighborhood we set fire to
Mrs. Gorman's chicken coop.

MY BULLY

he was big and he was always after me
down at the loading dock.
"I'm gonna kick your ass," he told me.
"listen, Jimmy, there are 50 guys out
here, why don't you kick somebody
else's ass?"
"no," he said, "I'm gonna kick *your*
ass."
well, I couldn't blame him.
there was something about me, a
lot of guys wanted to kick my ass, I'd
had that problem for years.
maybe I looked easy, maybe it was
because I was good-natured, liked to
clown around.
anyhow, I had a problem and it was
Jimmy, all 230 pounds of him.

it was midweek and we were
sitting around eating lunch out of our
brown bags
when Jimmy reached and
grabbed my sandwich.
"what the fuck is this?" he asked.
he took the sandwich in his
fist and crushed it into a
round ball.
then he rolled it on the ground.

"well, hell," I said, "I'm on a diet,
anyhow."
"a diet, huh?" said Jimmy.
he held up a big right hand and
doubled it up.
"maybe you'd like to eat my
fist?"
"hey, Jimmy baby, I'm no
cannibal."
"JUST SHUT UP!" he screamed.
I
shut up.

I don't know, he just kept after me
with his threats and somehow I
didn't feel like I deserved any of
it.

then management moved me to a
small office on the dock.
it was Sunday.
there was nothing to do, I just
answered the phone and tried to
look wise.

Jimmy was working that
Sunday.
he stood there glaring at me through
the glass partition.
then he began coming toward me.
I was feeling depressed, I had just
split with my shackjob.

Jimmy walked up.
"come on out of there, I'm going to beat
the shit out of you!" he said.
"all right, Jimmy," I said.
I came out and moved toward him, thinking,
I better get in a few shots fast because that's
all I've got time for.
he backed off a little and I caught him on
the nose with the first right.
his nose moved back into his head and spurted
red.
I'm dead now, I thought, and my left caught him
on the ear.
I put a right to his belly and it was soft, my fist
seemed to sink in half a foot.
Jimmy fell to the ground and held his face and
began sobbing like a
girl.

I looked around at the guys.
"what the fuck," I said, "this guy is a fake."

"Jesus," somebody said.

we all drifted away.
I went back to the office, sat down.
after a while Jimmy got up, walked down
to the end of the loading dock, jumped off, and
    disappeared
into the alley.

we never saw him again.

I never really understood what it all meant.
and nobody ever talked about him
to me again.
it was like it never
happened.

OW OW OW

    fellow runs a bookstore.
I go in there and sign my books for
  him
and he always forces a book on me
something about the rough-and-tumble
  life
but these books are written by
newspaper
  columnists
professors, born-into-wealthers,
  etc.
and these have seen about as much real
  low life
as a parish priest;
  their lives
have been about as adventuresome as
dusting a library
  shelf
and none of them has ever missed a
  meal.
these books are well written,
sometimes clever
just a touch
  daring
but there is an overriding sense
of comfort
in the writing and in the
  life.

the books fall from my
   hand.
this bookstore fellow is
going to have to think
of some other means of
   rewarding
me for
   signing my books
because reading this nicely
printed
   crap
only reminds me
once again
that I am competing only
against
   myself.

THE SINGERS

it was a Sunday night. I found a booth,
ordered a beer and dinner, and waited.
there were two musicians, a
man with a guitar and a woman who sang
with the man as he played.
they went from table to table, from booth to
booth, serenading the customers who were
mostly families with children.
the songs were popular melodies that I had
heard many times before and despised.
it was tired stuff, worn and played to death.
my dinner was slow in arriving and I ordered
another beer.
the singers finished at a table, then turned and
approached me.
I raised my hands, waved them off, said,
"no, no, no!"
they walked past to the booth behind me and
began.
they had wanted to share their
mediocre music with me
but I had warded them off.
I felt quite proud of my quick decision
to do so.

my dinner arrived and I ate in peace.

ten years ago, maybe even five, I would

have allowed the singers to descend on
me, but no longer.

often it takes a lifetime to learn how to
react to certain critical situations.
it's worth waiting for the arrival of maturity
and confidence.
try it sometime and see how delightful it
is to feel powerful and
alive.

THE MARCH

whenever I hear the *March to the
Gallows*
playing on the radio
I think of her
in that blue milkmaid's dress
that showed off her
figure
there in Santa Fe.
it was raining
the *March* was playing
the rain was pouring down
there were even candles
burning!
it was a large but
comfortable
house
and I told her what she
was doing to
me,
how much I
wanted her,
what a miracle it
was.
I was so poor and so
ugly
and there I was
with
her!

but I was also a
fool
and I loved my
wine
and I foolishly played the
foolish drunk as
the *March* played
on and on
in that warm room,
it would end, then
play once
again

I looked over
and there she was
on the couch,
absolutely
naked,
milk-
white.

an astonishing
frightening
and riveting
sight

"I'll be right there,"
I said, "just one more
drink."

I never made it
there.

she drove me to the
airport the
next day.

some months passed
and then there was a
letter from
her.

you looked so sad
on that drive to the airport.
I've thought of you often.
I bought a new car,
bright red, it's silly
but I can't think of the
name, you know, who
made it. it's raining now.
when it rains here it
rains like hell, remember?
oh, I'm gay now.
we live together, Doreen
and I. we have some
terrible arguments but
basically, I'm happy.
how are you?

THE WAY THINGS ARE

first they try to break you with grinding
poverty
then they try to break you with empty
fame.

if you will not be broken
by either
then there are natural methods
such as the usual diseases
followed by an unwelcome
death.

but most of us are broken long before
that
as it's meant to
be

by earthquake
flood
famine
rage
suicide
despair

or simply

by seriously
burning your nose
while lighting a
cigarette.

WORDS FOR YOU

red dogs in green hell, what is this
divided thing I call
myself?

what message is this I'm offering
here?

it's so easy to slide into
poetic pretension.

almost all art is shot through with
poetic
pretension:

painting
sculpting
the stage
music

what is this foolish
strutting and posturing
we do?

why do we embroider everything we say
with special emphasis

when all we really need to do
is simply say what
needs to be said?

of course
the fact is

that there is very little that needs
to be said.

so we dress up our
little artful musings
and clamor for attention
so that we may appear to be
a bit more
important
or even more
truthful
than the others.

what is this I'm writing
here?

what is this you're
reading here?

is it no worse than the rest?

probably even a little bit
better?

STRICTLY BULLSHIT

now
there's a *new* one
going around:
he is whining and
telling people
that
I
was responsible
for him
not getting
published
by
The Black Vulture Press.

there have been
at least
three other poets
who have whined about
this.

well, luckily, I
don't have time to
read unsolicited manuscripts
or
advise
The Black Vulture Press.

but
if I did
I would have rejected

all three
along with
at least a dozen
other
dandies
who would like to
be published
there.

that's why I would
never
edit or publish
any
literary
gang.

at least
at the track
I can bet
on something
that won't whine and complain
and will show me
some fight
and
some run.

WRITTEN BEFORE I GOT ONE

the best writers now
I'm told
have

word processors.

I'm not even sure what a
word processor
is.

but
no matter
the tree roots tangled
in my mother's bones

no matter
the shadows in the forgotten
canyon

no matter
the dream of the last
elephant

I'm not getting
one

whatever it
is

but
I hope it helps the best
writers get better

because I never could read them
anyhow.

and any boost for them
major or minor
will help us
all.

right?

STRAIGHT ON

there's nothing quite like driving the
hairpin curves on the Pasadena Freeway at 85
m.p.h.
hung over
checking the rearview mirror for officers of the
law
while peeling and eating tangerines that
sometimes
choke you with their
pulp, acid, seeds
as
your eyes fill with tears
your vision blurs
and you drive from memory
and on instinct
until
things get clear again.
finally you reach Santa Anita, that most beautiful race-
track,
and glide into the parking lot,
get
out, lock it, walk
in.

being 68 years old feels better than
30.
especially 30, that was the most depressing
birthday: you figured then that the gamble had been
lost.

what an awful
mistake you made then

38 years ago, about the time when they built
the
Pasadena Freeway.

REMEMBER THIS

believing what they say or write
is
dangerous
especially if they say or write
impossibly grand things
about
you

and you
are foolish enough to
believe them.

you are then apt to smash the
camera when somebody attempts to
photograph you in
public.

or you might get drunk
at your place
and shoot through the window
at your neighbor
with a
.44 magnum.

or you could purchase a very
expensive automobile
and then become irritated
with the less wealthy
in their old cars
who block your progress

on the
freeway.

or you might get married
too many times
or have too many
girlfriends.

or you could go to Europe
too often
or get high too
often.

you could
abuse
waiters.

refuse
autograph
seekers.

you could even
kill
somebody.

or
in a thousand
other ways
you could even finally
kill
yourself.

many
do.

NOW SEE HERE

playing with words as the mind fries and
pops like an egg left unattended in the
pan
while my cat crawls into a large paper bag
turns around
within and
looks out at me.

my woman is out tonight doing something
social.

I used to mind
I no longer mind.

if she can find pleasure
out there
I would say that
the world is better for
that.

the radio music is not very good
tonight
as I play with these words
as

I now
stare at
a red package of

50 white
envelopes.

what happened to those nights, man,
when you used to rip off poem after
poem?

oh shut up, I answer myself,
I don't feel at *all* like examining the
past, the present or the
future.

o.k., my brain says, I'm going on
strike too.

as my cat crawls out of the
paper bag
it's

a fairly slow night here.

LITTLE POEM

little sun little moon little dog
and a little to eat and a little to love
and a little to live for

in a little room
filled with little
mice
who gnaw and dance and run while I sleep
waiting for a little death
in the middle of a little morning

in a little city
in a little state
my little mother dead
my little father dead
in a little cemetery somewhere.

I have only
a little time
to tell you this:

watch out for
little death when he comes running

but like all the billions of little deaths
it will finally mean nothing and everything:

all your little tears burning like the dove,
wasted.

PART 2

real
loneliness
is not
necessarily
limited to
when
you are
alone.

GERTRUDE UP THE STAIRWAY, 1943

I think of Gertrude walking up that St. Louis
stairway
so many years ago
and myself just behind her
still almost a boy.
I think of Gertrude walking up that St. Louis
stairway
and never a stairway as taut with promise as
that one
with the landlady's pictures of Jesus
torn from cheap magazines
plastered here and there along the
walls.
I think of myself walking up that St. Louis
stairway
behind Gertrude
and into her room
going in there
the door closed firmly behind us
her pouring the claret
into tall thin glasses
in that dreary roominghouse
near that very large park
with its leafless trees of winter.
standing there
Gertrude seemed so lovely
so perfect
a girl beyond mere girlhood

a figure wrapped in a perfect
dream
and as
she stood there before me
she was finally
too perfect:
I downed my claret and begged my
leave
knowing that
following Gertrude up that St. Louis
stairway
was enough in
itself
it was
our one great moment together
and all that followed
would be
less
less
and I wanted to remember her like
that: perfect in the moment
before she wearied of the game and
we of each
other.

WHERE WAS I?

I didn't know where I came
from or where I was
going.
I was lost.
I used to sit
in strange doorways
for hours,
not thinking
not moving
until I was asked
to move.

I don't mean that I was an
idiot or a
fool.
what I mean is that
I was
uninterested.

I didn't care if you intended
to kill me.
I wouldn't stop you.

I was living an existence that
meant nothing to
me.

I found places to stay.
small rented rooms. bars. jails.
sleep and indifference seemed

the only
possibilities.

all else seemed
nonsense.

once I sat all night long and looked
out at the Mississippi River.
I don't know why.
the river ran by and
all I remember is that it
stank.

I always seemed to be
on a cross-country
bus
traveling
somewhere.
looking out a dirty
window at
nothing at
all.

I always knew exactly how much
money I was
carrying.
for example:
a five and two ones
in my wallet
and a nickel, a dime and
two pennies in my right
front pocket.

I had no desire to speak
to anybody nor to be
spoken to.
I was looked upon as a
misfit and a
freak.
I ate very little food but
I was amazingly
strong.
once, working in a factory
the young boys, the bruisers,
were trying to lift a heavy
piece of machinery from the
floor.
they all failed.

"hey, Hank, try it!" they
laughed.

I walked over, lifted it,
put it down,
went back to
work.

I gained their respect
for some reason
but I didn't want
it.

at times I would pull down
the shades in my room
and stay in bed for a
week or more.

I was on a strange journey
but it was
meaningless.
I had no ideas.
I had no plan.
I slept.
I just slept
and I waited.

I wasn't lonely.
I experienced no self-pity.
I was just caught up in a
life in which
I could find no
meaning.

then I was
a young man a
thousand years old.

and now I am an old man
waiting to be born.

SLOPPY DAY

I had been up until 3 a.m. the night before.
heavy drinking: beer, vodka, wine
and there I was at the track
on a Sunday.
it was hot.
everybody was there.
the killers, the insane, the fools.
the disciples of Jesus Christ.
the lovers of Mickey Mouse.
there were 50,000 of them.
the track was giving away
free caps
and 45,000 of those people were
wearing caps
and there weren't enough seats
and the crappers were crowded
and during the races
the people screamed so loud
that you couldn't hear the
track announcer over the loudspeaker and
the lines were so long
it took you
20 minutes to lay a bet and
between running to the crapper
and trying to bet
it was a day you
would rather begin
all over again

someplace else
but it was too late now and
there were elbows and assholes every-
where and
all the women looked vicious and ugly and
all the men looked stupid and ugly
and suddenly
I got a vision of
the whole mass of them copulating
in the infield
like death fucking death,
stinking and stale;
they were walking all around
belching, farting
bumping into each other
gasping
losing
lost
hating the dream
for not coming
true.

then
some fat son of a bitch with
a pink pig's head perched
on his body
came rushing up to me
(why?)
and while
I pretended to be looking away
and as he closed in

I dug my elbow into his gut.
I felt it sink in like he was
a sack of dirty
laundry.

"mother," he gasped,
help . . ."

"you all right, buddy?" I
asked.

he looked as if
he was going to puke.
his mouth opened.
he cupped his hand
and a pair of
yellow-and-pink false teeth
fell into his palm.

I walked on through the crowd
and found a betting line.
I decided to bet the last 5 races
and leave.
the only way I would stay
would be for $900 an hour
tax free.

20 minutes later
I had made my bets
and I walked out to the parking lot
and to my car.
I got in

opened the window and
took off my shoes.

then I noticed
that I was blocked in.
some guy had parked behind me
in the exit aisle.

I started my engine
put it in reverse and
jammed my bumper against him.
he had his hand brake on
but luckily he was in neutral and
I slowly ground him back up against
another car.
now the other car wouldn't be able
to get out.

what made that son of a bitch
do that?
didn't he have any
consideration?

I put my shoes on
got out
and let the air out of his
left front tire.

no good.
he probably had a spare.
so I let the air out of his
left rear tire
got back into my car and

maneuvered it out of there
with great difficulty.

it felt good to
drive out of that racetrack.
it sure as hell felt better than
my first piece of ass and
most of the other pieces
which followed.

I got to the freeway and
turned the radio on and
the man told me
I had just won
the first of my 5 bets.
the horse paid $12.40.
at ten-win that was
$52 profit so
I wasn't on skid row
yet.

by the time
I got to my driveway
the man on the radio told me
that my next horse had
run out.
they had sent in a $75 long shot.
too bad.

I parked in the garage
climbed out
put my key in the front door
kicked it open

got my blade out: over 50%
of home burglaries occur during the
day.
I checked the immediate
visible area
walked into the bathroom
pulled back the shower curtain:
nothing.

I walked out
stood in the front room
and then I heard a sound
in the kitchen
and I yelled,
"O.K., FUCKER, COME ON OUT AND
WE'LL SEE WHO'S BEST!"

there was no answer.

"ALL RIGHT, FUCKER, I'M COMING
IN!"

I ran into the kitchen with my
blade extended.

my cat was sitting up on the
breadboard.
he looked at me, amazed, then leaped off
and zoomed out of the kitchen.

I walked into the bedroom and
switched on the tube.
the Rams and Lions were
playing.

I kicked my shoes off, stretched out
on the bed, said, "shit."
got up again, went downstairs,
cracked a beer, came up, let the
bathwater run and
stretched out on the bed again.

the QB took the ball
dropped back
looked downfield to pass and
didn't see the big lineman
breaking in
from his left.
the lineman blindsided the QB
like a trash collection truck.

the QB was making $2 million a year
and he earned much of it
on that play.

he didn't get up.
he couldn't.
he didn't want to.

I could have been a football
player
only my father, that son of a
bitch, said that a man went to
school to study,
not play.

I flipped off the tv
disrobed and

walked into the bathroom.
I turned off the water
tested it with my hand.
nothing like a hot bath
in a cold world.
I got in
stretched out,
the 230 pounds of me
pushing the water
through the emergency drain.

son of a bitch,
why did they build
5-foot bathtubs
in a world of
6-foot people?

nobody knew anything
and they certainly weren't getting
any smarter.

NOTE ON THE TELEPHONE

often while I am up here
at the keyboard until 3 a.m.
or so
my wife gets on the telephone
downstairs
and conducts marathon
conversations
with her sister or her
niece
or somebody.
and as classical music
soothes my battered brain
and my fingers work
the keyboard
my wife works out
in her own way
on the telephone
discussing
for hours
whatever needs
to be discussed.
some seem to need this
kind of intercourse.
their very souls
seem to be
nourished
by an endless wave
of babble.

me, I'm just not a
telephone
person.

for me
it goes mostly
like this:
"sure. how are
you?
everything's
fine.
see you
later . . ."

I used to take
my telephone off
the hook
for days at
a time.
once I took
the damn
thing apart and stuffed the
bell and the
bell-ringer with
rags.
then I pissed on
it.

I believe
there's something
about the disembodied human
voice that

is not
reassuring.

you tell that to my wife
downstairs now and
she'll smile and say,
"have it your way!"

strange, isn't it?
how two such different people can
live under the same
roof

like
that.

AT THE EDGE

a smoky room at the edge, it's always
been a smoky room at the
edge.
the edge never goes away.
sometimes you understand it
better,
sometimes you even talk to it, you might
say, "hello, old friend,"
but it has no sense of humor, it slams you in the
gut, says,
"this is a serious business, I'm here to
kill you or drive you mad."
"all right," you reply, "I under-
stand."

tonight this room is smoky
and I am alone
listening to the silence.
I am tired of waiting on life,
it was so slow to arrive and so quick to
leave.
the streets and the cities are
empty,
love is on the damned cross
and death laughs in the back
room.

at the edge, the edge, the edge.

it's so sad: the flowers are still trying

to please me,
the sun shouts my name,
but my courage fails
as the animals look on with large
eyes.

this smoky room.
a stained rug.
a few books.
a painting or two.
a broken chair.
an empty pair of shoes.
a tired old man.

subordinated debt.

HEADS WITHOUT FACES,
SEEN IN ALL THE PLACES

to go mad, to suicide or to
continue?

sitting here now is
ridiculously perfect: there's
nothing to compare it
with.

a palsied past and a short
future.

on days like this
one can be depressed by
the message in a fortune
cookie.

november creeps in on all fours
like a leper.

there still might be a place
for us
somewhere.

it's not the doing
it's the waiting.

it's not the waiting
it's the waste.

it's not the waste
it's the durability of
the waste.

one who thus believes,
concedes.

COMING AWAKE

yawning and stretching,
putting on a clean pair of underwear
and thinking,
you are not in jail and you don't have
cancer
but there are probably a few people out there
who would like to murder you but they
probably won't actually come and do
it.
you think about how
you once decided to be buried
near Hollywood Park
so you could hear the horses pound by
as you slept
but lately they've talked about
moving Hollywood Park elsewhere
because the neighborhood has gotten
so poor
so now you must live longer
until you learn where they plan to
relocate.
putting on your shirt and pants
you remember that
you are being taught in some
contemporary literature courses
and you fart as you walk down
the stairway.
strange thoughts are much like
hangovers: you feel better
without them.

then you wonder if there's any coffee left as
you open the front door and look out
to see if your car has been
stolen.

THE SIMPLE TRUTH

you just don't know how to do it,
you know that,
and you can't do a lot of other
useful things either.
it's the fault of the
way you were raised,
some of it,
and you'll never learn now,
it's too late.
you just can't do certain things.
I could show you how to do them
but you still wouldn't do them
right.
I learned how to do a lot of necessary things
when I was a little girl
and I can still do them now.
I had good parents but
your parents never gave you enough
attention or love
so you never learned how to do
certain simple things.
I know it's not your fault but
I think you should be aware of how
limited you are.

here, let me do that!
now watch me!
see how easy it is!

take your time!
you have no patience!

now look at you!
you're mad, aren't you?
I can tell.
you think I can't tell?

I'm going downstairs now,
my favorite tv program is coming
on.

and don't be mad because
I tell you the simple truth about
yourself.

do you want anything from
downstairs?
a snack?
no?

are you sure?

HERE AND NOW

there are days
when it all goes
wrong.

on the freeway
at home
in the super-
market
and everywhere
else

continual
uninterrupted
ferocious
haphazard
assaults
on what
is left of
your
sanity and
sensibilities.

the gods first
play with you
and then
play
against
you.

your nerves

simmer until they're
raw.

no philosophical
shield
will protect you,
no amount of wisdom is
good enough.

you're hung out
as quarry
for the
dogs and
the
masses;
the breakdown
of the
machinery
and all
reason
is
total.

then
there's always
—suddenly—
a bright
smiling face
with dim
eyes, some
half-stranger
shouting

loudly:
"*hey, how ya
doing?*"

the face
all too close,
you see each
blemish and
pore in the
skin,
the loose
mouth is
like a broken
rotten
peach.

your only
thought
being,
shall I kill
him?

but then
you say,
"everything's
fine.
how about
you?"

and you
walk on past,
and the goat-
faced

half-stranger
is left
behind
as the sun
blazes down
through
acid
clouds.

you move
on
as the gods
laugh and
laugh
and
laugh,
you put one
foot
before the
other,
you swing your
arms
as the rusty
bell does
not ring,
as inside your
head
the blood
turns to
jello.

but
this day will end
this life will end
the vultures will
finally
fly
away.

please
hurry, hurry,
hurry.

CRAZY WORLD

fellow mailed me a knife in the mail.
said it was a gift in appreciation of my
work.
the knife has a lever on the side,
slide it and the blade shoots
out and you're ready,
fast.
I doubt if I'll ever use this weapon
but it's nice to have a reader who is that
concerned for my
safety.
but really, I prefer readers who mail me
bottles of wine
even if some of them arrive
broken.
still, you should never drink anything
sent through the mails from an unknown
individual, somebody might try to poison
you.
but anything is preferable to the reader who
arrives in person at the door.
this truly upsets and angers me.
in this world, even minor fame can be a
major problem.

anyhow, I'm now using the knife the reader
sent me to clean my fingernails.

better this than ripping it deep into
somebody's guts.

I prefer to do that with the
poem.

GOOD STUFF

Red had a job cleaning rooming
houses
and he often brought me the
relics of the dead.
"nobody wanted his stuff. look
at this shirt. you can't buy a
shirt like this anymore.
and try on these glasses."

"thanks, Red."

"here, try on this robe. look at
that god-damned thing. ever seen
anything like it?"

"no, no, I haven't."

"he died Tuesday. try it on."

I tried it on.
it was thick like a bed quilt—
heavy, and yellow and green.
I tightened the belt.

"it's too big for you but
it looks good. he was a big
guy. I knew him well. he worked as a
janitor and drank malt beer."

"thanks, Red, I can use this."

"need any stockings? underwear?"

"no, I'm all right there."

Red left to go clean more
rooms.

•

that big robe was like something that
kings wore in the old days.
I really liked it, I'd never seen
anything like it in the stores.
it must have been passed down from generation
to generation.

my new girlfriend came over that
night and we sat around drinking.
I was still at the stage where I was
trying to impress her.
so after drinking a couple of beers
I told her, "I'll be right back."

I went into the bedroom and put on the
robe and then walked out with my drink
in my hand.

"Jesus Christ, what's that?"

"this, my dear, is class!"

"it's too big and it's
filthy! where did you get
it?"

"some guy died and they were going
to throw it away."

I sat down next to her.

"it stinks!"

"there's nothing wrong with death," I
told her, "there is nothing shameful
about death."

I decided not to show her the shirt.
or my new pair of reading
glasses.

we didn't make love that night.

•

the next time Red came by he had a pair
of leather gloves.
"this guy died last Friday. he worked in a
box factory. his relatives came by
and cleaned the place out. but they
forgot these. I found them on the closet
floor."

I put them on.
they were a little small but they were
like new, just a tiny hole in the tip of
one finger, left hand.

"thanks, Red, they're beautiful!"

"you can't get gloves like that any
more."

"yes," I told him, "don't I know
it?"

RESPITE

fighting with women
playing the horses
drinking

sometimes I get too exhausted
to even feel bad

it's then that
listening to the radio
or reading a newspaper
is soothing,
comforting

the toilet looks kind
the bathtub looks kind
the faucets and the sink
look kind

I feel this way tonight

the sound of an airplane overhead
warms me
voices outside are
gentle and kind.

now I am content and
unashamed.

I watch my cigarette smoke
work up through the lamp shade
and all the people I have wronged
have forgiven me

but I know that I will go mad
again—
disgusted
frenzied
sick.

I need good nights like this
in between.
you need them too.

without them
no bridge would be
walkable.

THE HORSE PLAYER

I've been watching them for decades.
the jocks change but the horses
look about the same.
the mutuel clerks change, the parking lot attendants
    change
but the tracks do not.
I have seen two riders killed, half a hundred horses
    break
down.
I have had horses pay over $300 and less than $2.80.
I've seen them run in downpours
and in fog so thick that the announcer couldn't make
    the call.
I've bet on thoroughbreds, quarter horses, harness
    nags,
even the dogs.
I've watched them in Mexico and America and in
    Europe.
I've met women at the track and I've left women at
    the track.
I've attempted to make a living at the track and if you
    want
stress, there it is.
once I spent 3 months living near the track at different
    motels, sitting
alone in the bars at night.
I've had a half dozen winning systems and a half
    dozen losing

ones but, at the time, I couldn't tell which was
which.
finally I quit
with my tail between my legs, got a job and played
the horses on the side.

I have wasted a lifetime at the racetrack
and to this moment, I still go every day.
I don't know any other place to go.
the toteboard flashes and I move in.
I have no idea what I am looking for or what I expect
    to
find.
I speak to nobody.
I sit with my latest system and wait for the next
race.

what else can I do?

DISPLACED

burning in hell
this piece of me fits in nowhere
as other people find things
to do
with their time
places to go
with one another
things to say
to each other.

I am
burning in hell
some place north of Mexico.
flowers don't grow here.

I am not like
other people
other people are like
other people.

they are all alike:
joining
grouping
huddling
they are both
gleeful and content
and I am
burning in hell.

my heart is a thousand years old.

I am not like
other people.
I'd die on their picnic grounds
smothered by their flags
slugged by their songs
unloved by their soldiers
gored by their humor
murdered by their concern.

I am not like
other people.
I am
burning in hell.

the hell of
myself.

IN SEARCH OF A HERO

as far as literature is concerned,
for a while, it was Hemingway, then I
noticed that his writing was imitating itself, he was
not really writing anymore.

as far as sex is concerned,
I began quite late and being fully rested
I gave it a roaring start, learning more from each
    woman
and applying it in all its fulsome aspects to the next,
    awakening
in strange bed after strange bed (and then back in
    some old
beds) looking out the window in the morning to
    check
on my car parked outside—and remembering that
    there was
another woman for later that day and maybe even
    another one that
night.
dinners, lunches, walks in the park,
walks by the sea, sometimes unexpectedly a brother,
a son, an ex-husband and, once, a current husband.
I knew of nobody with as many girlfriends as I had
who was drinking as hard at the same time.
I was penniless and stupid
and almost without reason.
I'd return now and then to my tiny dirty room
to find wild notes under

my door and in the mailbox from
anxious females.
I had no time to respond and some then became
enraged,
trashing my automobile, breaking into my
room, destroying everything in sight, female
hurricanes from hell.
and the phone rang without pause throughout
all this carnage, curses, wails, hang-ups, callbacks,
threats of love, threats of death, and if I took
the phone off the hook for a bit, soon the sound of
a racing motor, the screeching of brakes
and then a rock thrown through the window.
3 times there was an attempted murder
despite the fact that
I was old and ugly, worse than poor,
often without even toilet paper in
the bathroom. but somehow
in my demented state
I became my own hero.

I'd go into Black bars,
I'd go into biker bars,
I'd go drunk into Mexican bars,
I'd go anywhere,
I'd spit into the eye of God and
even into the face of the devil.
then I'd wake up somewhere
with someone new
in the morning
and the sun would be

shining
as if for me alone.

I bought the cheapest junk cars
off the lots
and drove them to Caliente, to
Mexico,
the woman saying,
"Jesus, you're driving this thing
like a maniac!"
I'd squander my meager dollars at the race
track
with bravado
as if all the gods were
on my side.

it all ended
some place, somewhere,
in a small
room in downtown L.A.
I was there with this beautiful
girl with long hair, so
young, such a fine body, such
long long hair, it was almost all
too much. I think it began
in a bar downstairs or around
the corner and it was
arranged that I was to have
sex with this child of
unbelievable beauty
but there

was also a large heavy Mexican
woman there, even
uglier than I and I turned to her
and said, "you can leave the
room now."

"I stay," she said. "I make sure
you not hurt her."

Christ, she was ugly.
the cheap flowers on
the wallpaper bloomed and
blossomed at me.
I wanted the obvious to be
obvious.

I looked at the ugly woman.
"I don't want her," I heard myself say,
"I want you."

"huh?"

"I'm going to fuck *you*!"

I rushed at her,
noticing at the same
time that the beautiful girl on
the bed was not moving, was not interested,
was not saying anything.

the big woman was
stronger than I,
she fought me off,
it was a

battle, I reached for her
breast,
I tried to kiss her
wretched
mouth
but she was full of
refried beans and
good
old-fashioned strength,
we banged against the
dresser,
spun around,
she shoved me away,
I crashed against the wall,
she rushed at me
and swung a heavy arm at
the end of which was attached
a metal claw I
had not noticed.
no hand, just this gleaming,
metallic, dangerous
claw.
I ducked under the claw
and she swung again.
I leaped aside and
ran to the door to find
it shut tight.
I ducked under the swinging
claw once more.
you have no idea how it

glinted, glinted in the
cheap light that
illuminated that heartless
room.
I flung open the door and
ran down the stairway
and she chased me down.
and I ran out into the street,
I ran and I ran
and when I looked around
she was gone.
and then luckily for me,
unlike so many other nights,
elsewhere and everywhere,
I remembered
exactly where I had parked
my car.

the albatross is a fake,
the universe is a shoe,
there are no heroes,
there is only a mouse
in the corner
blinking its eyes,
there is only a corner
with a blinking mouse,
two toads embrace
what's left of the sun
as the monkey
manages a tired
smile.

ESCAPADE

the end of grace, the end of what matters.
the eye at the bottom of the bottle
is ours
winking back.
old voices, old songs are a
snake which crawls
away.

men go mad looking into empty faces.
why not?
what else is there for them to do?
I have done it.

the eye at the bottom of the bottle
winks back.
it's all a trick.
everything is an illusion.
there must be something better somewhere.
but where?
not here.
not there.

slowly one crawls toward imbecility,
welcoming it like a lost
lover.

I weary of this contest with myself
but it's the only sport in
town.

BURNING, BURNING

a dismal god-damned night, the birds are limp
on the wire, the cats asleep on their backs,
legs stuck up into the lifeless
air. the homeless are still
homeless as a bell rings in my head
and
on the radio a man
shoves a Spanish rhapsody by Liszt
at me like an insult.
then, that's over and I'm told that eventually
something by Bach will be along if I manage to
stay awake.
as if to help, boat horns now blast from the
harbor.
if it weren't so hot tonight those things would all
fit together but instead
there's a madness in the air.

letter from a fellow from England today, he writes
that I am one of the few people he
admires.
well, he hasn't met me personally.

and, something else: there are no daring lives anymore,
none at all.
the only daring activity left is when
we kill.
and I'm not preaching or suggesting.

I'm simply telling you how
it is.

I get cranky in the heat, drink too much, smoke bits
of old cigars, pull at my left ear, scratch my
arms, think of bellybuttons, tombstones, cacti,
watchsprings, other oddities.

well, look, here's Bach and I'm still awake.
I need another reason to stay in this room full of
ghosts,
some of them my own.
it could be worse, it will be.

nights like this. stuck here. grim reality
belches, more
boat horns blow.
the years hang strangled. I
burn my hand with a match.

the dream lies huddled, muddy.

confusion and sanctity reign.

effortless, painful, obnoxious, beautiful nights
like this. lives
like this.

there's too much to say, the dead
laugh as Bach enters
making palaces of sound, I can't stand it and yes
I can.

UPON READING AN INTERVIEW WITH A BEST-SELLING NOVELIST IN OUR METROPOLITAN DAILY NEWSPAPER

he talks like he writes
and he has a face like a dove, untouched by
externals.
a little shiver of horror runs through me as I read
about
his comfortable assured success.
"I am going to write an important novel next year,"
   he says.
next year?
I skip some paragraphs
but the interview goes on for two and one-half pages
more.
it's like milk spilled on a tablecloth, it's as soothing as
talcum powder, it's the bones of an eaten fish, it's a damp
stain on a faded necktie, it's a gathering hum.
this man is very fortunate that he is not standing
in line at a soup kitchen.
this man has no concept of failure because he is
paid so well for it.
I am lying on the bed, reading.
I drop the paper to the floor.
then I hear a sound.
it is a small fly buzzing.
I watch it flying, circling the room in an irregular
pattern.

life at last.

NOTHING TO IT

"now," said the doctor, "I am going to explain the entire procedure to you so you don't worry. we're going to run a little tube down into your lungs. there's a light on the end and we're going to look around. also there is a little clipper attached and it will take a snip here and there and bring some samples back so we can have them analyzed. the tubes are lubricated and slide right in. we enter one nostril, go down through the throat and into the lung. would you prefer we go in the left or the right nostril?"

"the left," I said.

"the left? fine. now we want you on your back. but first, maybe you'd like to look at the tubes?"

"no," I said.

"the whole procedure will be complete in from ten to fifteen minutes. we're going to have a little look, take a little snip, the tubes are lubricated, there's nothing to it."

I glanced at the tubes. they looked like battery cables.

"nurse," said the doctor.

"yes?" I said.

"no," said the doctor, "I was calling the
nurse."

"sorry," I said.

then I was on my back and two intent masked faces
   were bending
over me.

I had been on my way to the racetrack.
it was already past noon.
I was definitely going to miss the first
post.

THIS PLACE

twenty-five thousand fools
lined up for a free hamburger
at the racetrack today and
got it.

in 1889
Vincent entered a
mental asylum in
St. Remy.

1564: Michelangelo, Vesalius,
Calvin die; Shakespeare, Marlowe,
Galileo
born.

caught a flounder yesterday,
cooked it
today.

midst the din of this
imperfect life
a blinding flash of
light
tonight:
when I let the
6 cats in
it was so
perfectly
beautiful
that
for a
moment

I
turned away
and faced the east
wall.

A.D. 701–762

these dark nights
I begin to feel like
the Chinese poet
Li Po:
drinking wine and writing
poems
writing poems and drinking
wine

all the while
aware of the strict limitations
that come with
being
human

then
accepting that

the wine and the poems
gently
intermixing:

yes, there is a peaceable place
to be found
in this unending
war
we call life

where
things
such as
light, shadow, sound

objects
become
gently
and meaningfully
fascinating.

Li Po
drunk on his
wine
knew very well that
just to know
one thing well
was
best.

REGRETS OF A SORT

I've written all these poems
just using the words
I know
even when my writing sometimes
became almost like
listening to your
neighbor
over the
backyard fence.

but I do like
the music of language:
the curl of the unexpected
word
the sensation
of a
tasty
almost never-used
near-virgin
word.

there are so many
of them.

at times
I read the dictionary
marveling
at the immensity of
that untouched
backlog.

there's a force
there
that properly exploited
would make
all I've written
seem
terribly simple.

yet
when I consider
the many poets
who have delved into this immense
backlog:

the educated
the cultured
the
all-knowing

it
doesn't appear to have
worked
very well
for them.
perhaps have they
chosen
the wrong
words?
For the wrong
reasons?

or without
taste?

or the need to
communicate?
whatever,
the users
of exotic words
have discouraged me
from trying to use my
vocabulary
as if it was
a shield
for pretenders.

and so
for the moment
for now
I am caught
with this
left with
this

and since you
have come with me
this
far

so
are you.

TOO YOUNG

I worked for a while in a picture frame
factory where my job was to hand-sand
the wood before it was assembled and
painted.

another man sat at a machine and he
ran the wood through and chopped it
into various lengths.
he worked the cutting blade by
stamping down on a lever with his
right foot.

I watched him for several days, then
I walked up to him.
"Jesus Christ, is that all you do?
I mean, just pump your foot up and
down for 8 hours?
doesn't that drive you
crazy?"

the man didn't reply and I went back
to my hand-sanding.

after that the other workers didn't
speak to me.

ne week later the boss called me into
his office.
"we are going to have to let you
go."

he wrote out my check and I took it
and walked out of there.

outside as I walked along I felt
good, I felt that I understood something
very special.

about a month later
it was past midnight
and I was attempting to sleep
in a flophouse
alongside 35 or 40 men
on cots and
most of them were moaning
or snoring
loudly.

I still felt that I knew
something very special
which shows you
how little I really knew
at that particular
time.

LISTENING TO THE RADIO AT 1:35 A.M.

I switch the station:
a man plays the piano in grand
fashion.

somewhere else
there are nice homes
on the ocean shore
where you can
take your drink
out on the veranda
and
stand at ease and
watch the waves
listen to the waves
crashing in the dark
and yet
at the same time
you can feel crappy there
too

just like me now
having a dog fight
fighting for my life
within these 4 walls
20 miles inland.

UNCLASSICAL SYMPHONY

the cat murdered
in the middle of the street

tire-crushed

now it is nothing

and neither are
we

as
we
look
away.

DINNER FOR FREE

I was an unknown starving writer when I met this beautiful
lady who was young, educated, rich. I really can't
remember how it all came about. she had come by my destroyed
apartment a few times for brief visits. "I don't want sex,"
she told me. "I want you to understand that right from the start."
"o.k.," I said, "no sex."

one night she invited me to dinner (her treat). she
arrived in her new Porsche and we drove off.

the table was in front. it was a fancy place, and
there was a fellow with a violin and a fellow at the
piano.

I ordered wine and then we ordered dinner. it was quiet. too early
for the music, I guessed. it was good red wine.

the wine went quickly and I ordered another bottle.

"tell me about your writing," she said.

"no, no," I said.

the dinner arrived. I had ordered a porterhouse steak and fries.
she had something delicate. I don't remember what it was.

we began eating.

she started talking. it began easily enough. something
about an art exhibit. I nodded her on.

being an unknown starving writer it didn't take me
    very
long to clean my plate.

she began talking about the life of Mozart, slowly
    putting small
morsels of food into her mouth.

I poured more red wine.

then she started talking about saving the American
    Indian
from him/her self.

I quickly ordered another bottle of wine.

the waiter took our plates and she began pouring her
    own
wine and tossing it down.

she told me that Immanuel Kant had a most brilliant
    mind,
astonishingly brilliant.

as we sat her voice got louder and louder. she spoke
more and more rapidly.

then the guy at the piano started playing and the guy
    with the
violin joined in.

she raised her voice even more to be heard over the
   music.

she was back to saving the American Indian from
   him/her self.

I began getting a headache. as I sat and listened to her
my headache got worse.

she began to explain what Jean Paul Sartre really
meant.
the guy at the piano and the guy with the violin
   began to play louder
and louder to be heard over her.

finally I waved my arms at her and yelled, "LOOK,
   LET'S GO
   BACK TO MY
   PLACE!"

she paid the bill and I got her out of there. she talked
   all
the way back to my place. we parked and went in.

I had some scotch. I poured the scotch. I sat on the
   couch and
she sat on a chair across the room, talking loudly and
rapidly.

she was talking about Vivaldi, on and on about Vivaldi.

then she stopped to light a cigarette and I spoke.

"look," I told her, "I really don't want to fuck you."

she jumped up, knocked over her drink, began
     prancing around the
room. "oh, hahaha! I *know* you really want to fuck
     me!"

then she went into some type of energetic dance,
     holding her
cigarette over her head. she was very awkward,
     breathing
heavily and staring at me in a peculiar way.

"I have a headache," I told her. "I just want to go to
     bed and to
sleep."

"haha! you're trying to trick me into your bed!"

then she sat down and looked at me, still breathing
     heavily.

"I'm not going to let you fuck me!"

"please don't," I said.

"tell me about your writing," she said.

"look," I said, "will you please just get out of here and
     leave
me alone?"

"ha!" she jumped up.

"ha! you men are all alike! all you think about is
fucking!"

"I don't have the slightest desire to fuck you," I said.

"ha! you expect me to *believe* that?"

she grabbed her purse, ran to the door. then she was out the
door, slamming it behind her.

and just like that, my beautiful, young, rich, educated lady
was gone.

A SONG FROM THE 70'S

Hank, about the voices I hear, they talk to
me whenever I get in a medication jam like
I'm in now; I'm out of Valium and can't get any
until tomorrow.
I'm supposed to take Navane twice a day, one
at breakfast and one at bedtime plus three
Desyrel, one in the morning and two in the evening
plus 15 mg. of Valium a day, one tab usually around 9
in
the morning, one at 2 in the afternoon, one at 5 and
one
before I go to sleep but I like to get high and usually
take 3 at a time.
I ran across a couple of old prescriptions for codeine
and
Percodan last week and I took 40 codeines and 20
Percodans in 6 days. because I was
loaded I thought I threw the Percodan
prescription into the dumpster and scrounged
around in there for 30 minutes before I
discovered I had hidden it in my underwear so
my mother wouldn't find it.

I fell out of bed a few weeks ago and there was
this terrible black-and-blue mark on my leg near
my butt, so my mother made me go to the
Emergency Ward at Presbyterian Hospital and a young
intern there drew a circle around the mark with a
felt pen and gave me 30 tabs of Percodan and a

synthetic morphine shot, then I went to see my
internist and he looked at the black-and-blue mark
with the circle drawn around it and he wrote another
prescription for 40 more codeines.

I say legalize drugs for Christ's sake, and bring
back Country Joe and the Fish!

.188

it dissolves, it all dissolves: those we thought
were great, so exceptional—they dissolve;
even the cat
walking across the rug vanishes in a
puff of smoke;
nations break apart at the seams
and overnight become
tenth-rate powers;
the .330 hitter can no longer
see the ball, he dips to .188,
sits apart on the bench,
wonders about
the remainder of his life;
the heavyweight champ is knocked senseless by
a 40-to-one underdog;
it dissolves, it all dissolves—
lovers leave and
old cars break down
on the freeway at rush hour;
I look at a photo of myself
and think,
who's that
awkward
foolish
old man?
it dissolves—the nights of hurricane and
hunger

have turned
placid;
I search for a partial set of my teeth
on the bookcase
shelf;
and I can't even think of
a last line
for this poem;
sometimes
before his death
a man can see
his
ghost.

WAR SOME OF THE TIME

when you write a poem it
needn't be intense
it
can be nice and
easy
and you shouldn't necessarily
be
concerned only with things like anger or
love or need;
at any moment the
greatest accomplishment might be to simply
get
up and tap the handle
on that leaking toilet;
I've
done that twice now while typing
this
and now the toilet is
quiet.
to
solve simple problems: that's
the most
satisfying thing, it
gives you a chance and it
gives everything else a chance
too.

we were made to accomplish the easy
things
and made to live through the things that are
hard.

AT LAST

I am sitting here
in darkest night
as one more poem
arrives
and says
wait,
wait,
watch me as I strut
across the page
letter by letter
like one of your
cats
walking across the
hood of your
car.
watch me,
here I
go
again
all the way to
Mexico
or Java
or down
into your
gut.
wait
some
more,

these nights
are meant for that,
and for
me
because
I control
you,
a captive there
sitting before
this
illuminated
screen.
you will do as I
want
because
I write
you,
not the other
way around.
I always have.
I always will.
I am the last
poem of this
night
and as you
sleep later in the
next room
in the dark
you will
forget about

me,
forget everything,
you with your
dumb mouth
open,
as you snore your
heavy
sleep,
I will be here
waiting,
immortal,
and
when you are
dead
and the black
sky flashes
red
for you
for the last time,
your dumb
bones
will amount to
nothing
more
than
dust.
but I will
live on.

MISBEGOTTEN PARADISE

the bad days and the bad nights now come too
often,
the old dream of having a few easy
years before death—
that dream vanished as the other dreams
have.
too bad, too bad, too bad.
from the beginning, through the
middle years and up to the
end:
too bad, too bad, too bad.

there were moments,
sparkles of hope
but they quickly dissolved
back into the same old
formula:
the stink of reality.

even when luck was
there
and life danced in the
flesh,
we knew the stay
would be
short.

too bad, too bad, too bad.

we wanted more than
there could ever be:

women of love and
laughter,
nights wild enough for the
tiger,
we wanted days that
strolled through
life
with some grace,
a bit of
meaning,
a plausible use,
not something
just to
waste,
but something to
remember,
something
with which to
poke death
in the gut.

too bad, too bad, too bad.

in the totality of
all things, of course,
our petty agony is
stupid
and vain
but I feel that our
dreams were
not.

and we are not alone.
the relentless factors are
not a personal
vendetta against a
single
self.

others feel the same
searing
disorder,
go mad, suicide, go
dull, run stricken to
imaginary
gods,
or go drunk, go drugged,
go naturally
silly,
disappear into the mass of
nothingness
we call families,
cities,
countries.

but fate is not entirely
to blame.
we have wasted
our chances,
we have strangled
our own hearts.

too bad, too bad, too bad.

now we are the citizens of
nothing.

the sun
itself
knows
the sad truth of
how we surrendered
our lives
and deaths
to simple
ritual,
useless
craven
ritual,
and then
slinking away
from the face of
glory,
turning our dreams into
dung,
how we said
no, no, no, no,
to the most beautiful
YES
ever uttered:

life
itself.

MY BIG NIGHT ON THE TOWN

sitting on a 2nd-floor porch at 1:30 a.m.
while
looking out over the city.
it could be worse.

we needn't accomplish great things, we only
need to accomplish little things that make us feel
better or
not so bad.

of course, sometimes the fates will
not allow us to do
this.

then, we must outwit the fates.

we must be patient with the gods.
they like to have fun,
they like to play with us.
they like to test us.
they like to tell us that we are weak
and stupid, that we are
finished.

the gods need to be amused.
we are their toys.

as I sit on the porch a bird begins
to serenade me from a tree nearby in
the dark.

it is a mockingbird.

I am in love with mockingbirds.
I make bird sounds.
he waits.
then he makes them back.

he is so good that I laugh.

we are all so easily pleased,
all of us living things.

now a slight drizzle begins to
fall.
little chill drops fall on my
hot skin.

I am half asleep.
I sit in a folding chair with my
feet up on the railing
as the mockingbird begins
to repeat every bird song
he has heard that
day.

this is what we old guys do
for amusement
on Saturday
nights:
we laugh at the gods, we
settle old scores with
them,
we rejuvenate
as the lights of the city
blink below,

as the dark tree
holding the mockingbird
watches over us,
and as the world,
from here,
looks as good as it ever
will.

NOBODY BUT YOU

nobody can save you but
yourself.
you will be put again and again
into nearly impossible
situations.
they will attempt again and again
through subterfuge, guise and
force
to make you submit, quit and/or die quietly
inside.

nobody can save you but
yourself
and it will be easy enough to fail
so very easily
but don't, don't, don't.
just watch them.
listen to them.
do you want to be like *that*?
a faceless, mindless, heartless
being?
do you want to experience
death before death?

nobody can save you but
yourself
and you're worth saving.
it's a war not easily won

but if anything is worth winning then
this is it.

think about it.
think about saving your self.
your spiritual self.
your gut self.
your singing magical self and
your beautiful self.
save it.
don't join the dead-in-spirit.

maintain your self
with humor and grace
and finally
if necessary
wager your life as you struggle,
damn the odds, damn
the price.

only you can save your
self.

do it! do it!

then you'll know exactly what
I am talking about.

LIKE A DOLPHIN

dying has its rough edge.
no escaping now.
the warden has his eye on me.
his bad eye.
I'm doing hard time now.
in solitary.
locked down.
I'm not the first nor the last.
I'm just telling you how it is.
I sit in my own shadow now.
the face of the people grows dim.
the old songs still play.
hand to my chin, I dream of
nothing while my lost childhood
leaps like a dolphin
in the frozen sea.